William Shakespeare
Poet and Playwright

Stewart Ross

HODDER
Wayland
an imprint of Hodder Children's Books

© 2003 White-Thomson Publishing Ltd

Produced by White-Thomson Publishing Ltd
2/3 St Andrew's Place, Lewes, BN7 1UP

Editor: Elaine Fuoco-Lang
Inside and cover design: Tim Mayer
Picture Research: Shelley Noronha –
    Glass Onion Pictures
Proofreader: Jane Colgan

Cover: A portrait of William Shakespeare.
Title page: This picture appears on Shakespeare's collection
of works called the *First Folio*.

Published in Great Britain in 2003 by Hodder Wayland,
an imprint of Hodder Children's Books

British Library Cataloguing in Publication Data
Ross, Stewart
    Shakespeare. - (Famous lives)
    1.Shakespeare, William, 1564-1616 - Juvenile literature
    2.Dramatists, English - Early modern, 1500-1700 -
    biography - Juvenile literature
    I.Title
    822.3'3

ISBN 0 7502 4319 8

Printed in Hong Kong

Hodder Children's Books
An imprint of Hodder Headline Limited
338 Euston Road, London, NW1 3BH

Picture acknowledgements:
Bridgeman Art Library 8, 13, 14, 16, 17, 18, 20, 21, 23,
25, 27, 40, 43; Hodder Wayland Picture Library title page,
7, 9, 11, 24, 28, 29, 34, 37, 42; Mary Evans 6, 10, 19, 32,
41; National Portrait Gallery cover, 5, 30; National Trust
31; Pictorial Press 36, 38, 39, 45; The Globe
Theatre/Donald Cooper 22, 33; The Globe
Theatre/Richard Kalina 4; The Globe Theatre/John
Tramper 26, 35, 44; The Tate Gallery 15; Victoria and
Albert Museum, London, UK/Bridgeman Art Library 12.

Contents

At the Theatre

London, 1595. Two o'clock on a warm afternoon in early September. A large crowd is hurrying into The Theatre, a tall, many-sided playhouse just to the north of the city walls. It is currently showing a very popular new play, the tragedy of *Romeo and Juliet*.

> **'But soft! What light through yonder window breaks? It is the East, and Juliet is the sun!'**
> (Romeo's reaction to seeing Juliet, in the famous 'Balcony scene'. *Romeo and Juliet*, Act II, scene ii.)

The Globe Theatre was reconstructed during the 1990s close to the site of the original building in which many of William's finest plays were first performed.

When the gatherers at the doors have admitted the last of the audience — some seated, some standing in the space before the projecting stage — the doors are closed and the play begins.

4

This portrait of William Shakespeare painted after his death is based upon the only picture we have of him while he was alive (see page 37).

Curtains at the back of the stage draw apart. A man walks swiftly forward and raises his hands. As the noise within The Theatre dies down, he begins to speak:

> 'Two households, both alike in dignity,
> In fair Verona, where we lay our scene ...'

The members of the audience listen carefully, sure they're in for an enjoyable afternoon. After all, the play is from the pen of William Shakespeare, the most able young playwright of his generation.

Elizabethan England

William Shakespeare was baptised into the Church of England at Holy Trinity Church in Stratford-upon-Avon on 26 April 1564. Tradition says he was born on 23 April: St George's Day.

Not knowing William's exact birthday is typical of the difficulties faced by those piecing together his life. Only a small amount of exact information exists. The rest of his story has to be filled in as best we can. There is even a tiny minority of scholars who believe William did not write the plays and poems attributed to him. They suggest different authors, such as Christopher Marlowe and Edward de Vere, Earl of Oxford.

Where it all began: the room in the Shakespeares' house in Stratford-upon-Avon where William was supposed to have been born.

The glittering hub of the court: Queen Elizabeth I dancing.

'This royal throne of kings, this scept'red isle,
This earth of majesty, this seat of Mars,
This other Eden, demi-paradise ...
This blessed plot, this earth, this realm, this England.'
Richard II, Act II, scene i.

William's England (Scotland was then a separate country) was ruled by Queen Elizabeth I. She was assisted by courtiers, ministers, bishops and occasional parliaments. The kingdom was a vigorous, rowdy, rural land with three million inhabitants. It was proud of its independence and, increasingly, of its Protestantism.

7

The Shakespeares

William was born into a well-off, respectable family. His mother, Mary Arden, came from an ancient family who owned land in Warwickshire. His father, John Shakespeare, was a manufacturer of fine leather goods such as belts, purses and gloves.

The family lived in Henley Street in Stratford. Their three-storey, half-timbered house is still standing, although it has been altered since William's day.

The Arden family house in Wilmcote, Warwickshire, built in the early sixteenth century, where William's mother Mary was brought up.

**Who will buy?
A sixteenth-century
market scene.**

'When icicles hang by the wall,
And Dick the shepherd blows his nail ...
Then nightly sings the staring owl,
Tu-who;
Tu-whit, tu-who - a merry note,
While greasy Joan doth keel [cool] the pot.'
Is 'greasy Joan' Shakespeare's joke with his
sister? *Love's Labour's Lost*, Act V, scene ii.

John Shakespeare was a well-known figure in the small market town. He worked his way up to become bailiff, which was similar to mayor. Later, in William's teens, the family fortunes declined and John was forced to sell property. This may have made William more determined to make a success of his own life.

William was the oldest of John and Mary Shakespeare's surviving children. Two older sisters and one younger sister died young. His three younger brothers were Gilbert, Edmund and Richard. Joan was his only sister.

9

Learning and Faith

There is no record of William attending school. However, it is impossible that someone of his learning had received no formal education. It is believed that he went to Stratford-upon-Avon's grammar school.

The school, which gave a free education to the boys of the town's leading families, had a good reputation. Compared with today, the syllabus was very narrow. It was based around reading and writing Latin. Latin was regarded as the language of learning and was needed to enter university.

John Aubrey noted that some said William was ill-educated: *'... as Ben Jonson [a fellow playwright] sayes of him, that he had little Latine and lesse Greek.'* In *Brief Lives*.

Elizabethan England was scarred by religious bitterness. The national Protestant church, the Church of England, had recently split from the Roman Catholic Church. The government made life tough for Roman Catholics by fining them if they failed to attend Anglican church services.

A drawing from 1906 of the old grammar school at Stratford-upon-Avon where William was almost certainly educated.

*A page from **Sir Thomas More**, the play written by several authors, is believed to be a rare example of William's handwriting.*

William was baptised into the Church of England. But some scholars believe he and his father were secret Roman Catholics. In fact, William's plays give few clues about his private thoughts and feelings, so his religious beliefs remain a mystery.

The Teenage Mystery

Almost nothing is known for certain of the teenage William Shakespeare, although there are many legends. One says he was a schoolmaster for a few years. When John Shakespeare fell on hard times in 1576, he needed all the help he could get. The seventeenth century gossip and biographer, John Aubrey, said William worked for his father at this time.

'... when he [William] was a boy he exercised [worked at] his father's trade, but when he kill'd a calfe he would do it in high style, and make a speech.'
John Aubrey talks of William's childhood in *Brief Lives*.

The height of fashion: a miniature painting by Nicholas Hilliard of a young gentleman. It was completed around 1588, roughly when William came to London.

It is almost certain that in his youth William saw troupes of travelling actors who visited Stratford. These included French or Italians performing *commedia dell'arte*, a fashionable European style of drama that was popular from the sixteenth to the eighteenth century. It is the distant ancestor of English Punch and Judy shows.

A sixteenth-century performance of commedia dell'arte, the European drama that influenced the young Shakespeare.

English players performed morality plays. As their title suggests, these were tales designed to show how honest people were successful and those who were wicked were punished. We can see that William was influenced by both *commedia dell'arte* and morality plays in his work.

Marriage

In November 1582 Shakespeare was married. His bride was the 26-year-old Anne Hathaway, who was eight years older than him.

A late nineteenth-century painting of the cottage in which Anne Hathaway lived before her marriage to Shakespeare in 1582.

A seventeenth-century painting showing two sisters who have wrapped their babies in tight sheets, a process known as swaddling. It is likely that Shakespeare's babies would have been 'swaddled' like this.

'... in order to settle in the world after [in] a family manner, he thought fit to marry while he was yet very young. His wife was the daughter of one Hathaway, said to have been a substantial yeoman in the neighbourhood of Stratford.'
Nicholas Rowe, cited in G. B. Harrison's *Introducing Shakespeare*.

Nicholas Rowe, who wrote the earliest biography of William in 1709, says that Anne came from a well-off family. Her parents may have insisted that William marry her. She was pregnant, and in those days it was not respectable for an unmarried woman to have a baby.

The couple's first child, Susanna, was christened in May 1583. Rowe says she was William's favourite. Twins, Hamnet and Judith, were born in 1585.

Many years after William's death, rumours spread about how he had relationships with other women. Whether William loved Anne or not, at some time in his twenties he left his wife and family in Stratford and travelled down to London.

The Lost Years

The period 1585-92 is known as William Shakespeare's 'Lost Years'. In 1585 he was living in Stratford with Anne and the children, and by 1592 he was making a name for himself as a writer in London.

Party time! A public celebration in the village of Bermondsey, London in 1570.

Many suggestions have been made about why William left home. Some say he was bored with Stratford and family life and joined a troupe of travelling actors. He was a capable actor as well as a brilliant playwright.

Deer poaching, 1590. It is believed that the young Shakespeare may have tried his hand at this illegal sport.

John Aubrey had heard that William was *'a handsome, well-shap't man: very good company ...'* In *Brief Lives*.

The most exciting story about William's 'Lost Years' comes from Nicholas Rowe. He says that William and his young friends used to go poaching deer. A local landlord, Sir Thomas Lucy, caught William and had him harshly punished.

William took his revenge, says Rowe, by writing a mocking poem about Sir Thomas. The knight was so furious that William had to flee from Stratford to save his skin.

London and the Theatre

The population of England in the late sixteenth century was approaching four million. Over 200,000 people lived in London, by far the largest city in the kingdom. Unlike today, most of the city was on the north bank of the River Thames. Furthermore, it was a city of two distinct parts: the old crowded and walled 'city' in the east, dominated by the Tower of London and St Paul's Cathedral, and the cathedral and royal palace of Westminster in the west.

London in about 1572. Note the old walled city in the centre and the newer suburb of Westminster to the left (west).

18

Working in a playhouse was not an obvious choice of profession. It was not very respectable. Officials such as magistrates disliked plays because they attracted crowds. Any large gathering of people might become rowdy if stirred up by a speaker complaining about, say, taxes. Crowds also allowed diseases to spread. Puritans condemned acting as falsehood and deception. For years people had regarded travelling actors with deep suspicion.

However, putting on plays in purpose-built playhouses was new and exciting. It was the latest thing in the entertainment business, and the young William obviously enjoyed it.

A Victorian recreation of what a performance of Shakespeare's A Midsummer Night's Dream may have looked like in the author's day.

Working in the Playhouse

William did not just turn up in London and start acting or writing plays. It is believed that he first worked as a 'prompter's attendant', helping the man who sat at the side of the stage and reminded actors when they forgot their words. Another source says he held the horses of wealthy theatregoers while they went to the show.

'There is a tradition that his [William's] first office [job] in the theatre was that of prompter's attendant ... [telling] the performers ... to be ready to enter ... the stage.'
Malone, cited in G.B. Harrison, *Life of William Shakespeare.*

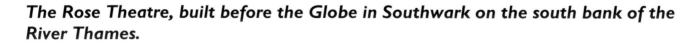

The Rose Theatre, built before the Globe in Southwark on the south bank of the River Thames.

RENTISSIMA BRITANN

THAMESIS

London in the late 16th century showing the Swan, Rose and Globe theatres, and the old St Paul's Cathedral (destroyed in the Great Fire of 1666) in the background.

There were two types of playhouse at the time: halls and amphitheatres. Barn-shaped hall playhouses held perhaps 150-250 people. The play was performed on a stage at one end. The audience was indoors and seats were expensive.

Amphitheatres, new to London, were round or oval and open to the air. The audience of 2,000 or more surrounded the stage on three sides. At playhouses of this type, such as the Rose Theatre, a standing place cost only one penny.

Plays were performed with little or no scenery and in Elizabethan costume. There were no actresses in William's time and female roles were played by boys.

A New Talent

By 1592 the 28-year-old William was an important member of London's theatre community. He was acting and writing so successfully that one of his rivals, Robert Greene, wrote a piece criticising him (see panel).

William's first drama: a modern production of **The Comedy of Errors** *in the reconstructed Globe Theatre in 1999.*

'*... there is an upstart [jumped up] crow ... supposes he is as well able to bombast [trumpet] out a blank verse as the best of you ...*"
Robert Greene, cited in Russ McDonald, *The Bedford Companion to Shakespeare.*

The great Victorian actress Sarah Bernhardt playing the prince in a production of Shakespeare's Hamlet *in 1899 at the Adelphi Theatre.*

William was not just a genius, but a genius in the right place at the right time. Theatres and serious playwriting in English was new, so he was able to explore their many exciting possibilities. Nor did he have to worry about borrowing a story that another playwright had used. His working of *Hamlet* (1600-02), for example, was a rewriting of an anonymous earlier work, based on a Norse legend and performed in London in 1589. The English language, too, was youthful, flexible and fresh, a green branch for William to twist and weave into magical patterns.

The Lord Chamberlain's Men

Plays were written for companies of actors. It is not certain for which companies William wrote his first plays – *The Comedy of Errors* (1588-93) and three parts of *Henry VI* (1588-92) – but they were very popular.

In 1593, following a serious outbreak of the bubonic plague, a killer disease, the London playhouses were closed. People who worked for the playhouses had to find work elsewhere. Luckily for William he was helped by his wealthy young noble patron, the Earl of Southampton. Perhaps at the earl's request, he wrote two long poems, *Venus and Adonis* and *The Rape of Lucrece*. These were printed and reprinted for public sale many times during William's lifetime.

A seventeenth-century portrait of Richard Burbage, the actor and businessman who worked closely with William for many years.

When the playhouses reopened, William returned to his normal work. He soon joined the actor-manager Richard Burbage in a new company called the Lord Chamberlain's Men. It took its name from the title of its patron, the Lord Chamberlain. Within a couple of years William had given the company a string of highly successful plays, including *Romeo and Juliet* (1594-96), *A Midsummer Night's Dream* (1594-96) and *Richard II* (1595).

Death (represented by skeletons) haunts Londoners as they flee their city to escape the plague.

Plays for All

By the mid-1590s William's plays were being performed at court. We are told that Elizabeth I so liked the character of Sir John Falstaff, who appeared in the First and Second parts of *Henry IV*, that she asked William to write a play about him. At royal command, the playwright wrote *The Merry Wives of Windsor* (1597-1600).

William's plays were remarkably popular. They were appreciated not just at court but by lawyers, merchants, working people, men, women, young and old. The range of his characters is magnificent, from romantic lovers (Romeo and Juliet) and worried kings (Henry IV) to overweight crooks (Falstaff), ambitious generals (Julius Caesar), naughty sprites (Puck) and drunken doorkeepers (in *Macbeth*).

A performance of **The Merchant of Venice** at the Globe Theatre in 1998.

'Hath not a Jew eyes? Hath not a Jew hands, organs, dimensions, senses, afflictions, passions? Fed with the same food, hurt with the same weapons ... warmed and cooled by the same winter and summer, as Christian is?'
(*The Merchant of Venice*, Act III, scene i.)

By the end of the century, having followed his early dramas with such masterpieces as *The Merchant of Venice* (1596-7) and *Much Ado About Nothing* (1598-9), he was already Europe's leading playwright.

In 1599, helped by the success of William's plays, the Lord Chamberlain's Men built a playhouse of their own. This was the Globe, across the River Thames from the City of London. Today a reconstruction stands near the original site.

As it was: a rare picture of the original Globe Theatre that burned down in 1613.

The Gentleman

As a member of the Lord Chamberlain's Men and its chief playwright, William was becoming a wealthy man. For much of 1590 William lived near The Theatre in London. It was here that he probably wrote his plays (about two a year). He also spent time in his home town of Stratford-upon-Avon. His family remained there and he was still deeply attached to the place.

Modern monument: the Shakespeare Memorial Theatre at Stratford-upon-Avon.

"He was wont [used] to goe to his native Countrey [birthplace] once a yeare. I thinke I have been told that he left 2 or 300 pounds per annum [a year].' John Aubrey in *Brief Lives.*

Modern costumes used for productions of William's plays. In the playwright's day the costumes were much simpler, with perhaps only one item representing a character's position in society.

Personally, 1596 was a bitter-sweet year. William was granted the right to have a coat of arms and call himself a gentleman. This was very prestigious in Elizabethan times. In the same year, however, William's only son, Hamnet, died. Perhaps William's play *Hamlet* (1600-2) was a tribute to his lost son?

In 1597 William bought New Place, a grand house near the centre of Stratford. As the town's second largest dwelling, it was a sure sign that William Shakespeare was becoming wealthy as well as successful.

A King's Man

At the turn of the century great changes occurred in William's life. His father died in 1601, followed two years later by Queen Elizabeth I. The new monarch was her cousin, King James VI of Scotland, who ruled England as James I.

The Lord Chamberlain's Men moved quickly to keep in good standing with King James. A well-educated man of high intelligence, he agreed to replace the Lord Chamberlain as patron of Shakespeare's theatre company. From now on it was known as the King's Men.

King James VI of Scotland and I of England, one of the best-educated monarchs to sit on the English throne, was a patron of William's theatre company.

"All hail, Macbeth!" Henry Fuseli's interpretation of Act I, scene iii, where the three witches tempt the heroic general in the play that bears his name.

Just as William had worked to please Elizabeth, he used his talent to impress the new king. In 1605-6 he wrote *Macbeth*, one of his best-known plays and the only one set in Scotland.

When *Macbeth* was played at court, King James was delighted by its Scottish setting. Moreover, the play featured witches, which fascinated him (he had written a book, *Daemonologie*, in 1597, on the subject of witchcraft). The play was also full of glowing references to the king's Scottish ancestors.

The Master

What is it about William's plays that makes them so special? First, he tells gripping stories. The plots of some early plays, like *The Comedy of Errors* (1588-93), are very complicated but in later ones the story-lines are much easier to follow.

Second, William created unforgettable characters. They are real individuals with distinct personalities and everyday strengths and weaknesses, hopes, doubts and fears. Some, like Queen Elizabeth's favourite, Falstaff, are amusing. Others, like Macbeth, King Lear and Hamlet, are tragic.

*A painting of the roguish Sir John Falstaff played by Herbert Beerbohm Tree in **The Merry Wives of Windsor**, a play that William was supposed to have written in less than two weeks.*

Julian Glover as King Lear, at the Globe Theatre in 2001, one of William's most brilliantly tragic plays.

Even famous villains, such as Iago in *Othello* (1604), and heroes, such as the king in *Henry V* (1599), are not simply villains and heroes. Their words and actions allow us to understand why they think and behave as they do.

William's famous phrases are sometimes used today: **'To be, or not to be', 'Parting is such sweet sorrow', 'A horse! A horse! My kingdom for a horse!'**
Hamlet, Romeo and Juliet, Richard III.

There is also William's magnificent language. He uses language in a way that makes it musical, rich and also to the point. His plays are mainly written in blank verse, known as 'iambic pentameters':

Methinks I am a prophet new inspired ...
[John of Gaunt in *Richard II*, Act II, scene i].

33

The Man of Property

After 1606, William's rate of work slowed down. In the ten previous years he had written about sixteen plays. Over the next ten years he wrote only about seven.

William was concentrating more on his business. He had always earned most from being a King's Men shareholder, and the company was flourishing. After the Globe, in 1608 the company opened the Blackfriars indoor playhouse. With his share of the company's profits, William bought land and further property in Stratford and, in 1612, a London house in Blackfriars.

People in Shakespeare's day didn't just go to the theatre to watch plays. Amongst the theatres on the south bank of the River Thames, almost directly opposite Blackfriars playhouse, was the bear garden where dogs attacked bears for the amusement of the spectators.

Mark Rylance as the prince with Joanna McCallum as Gertrude, his mother, in a famous modern production of Hamlet at the new Globe Theatre in 2000.

William no longer needed an individual patron, as the Earl of Southampton had been. Moreover, he had stopped writing non-theatrical poetry, such as *Venus and Adonis* and his sonnets. Although much of his personal life remains unclear, we can see from how he spent his money that a strong ambition drove him. He was eager to climb up the social ladder and enjoy a life of comfortable ease as a respected gentleman.

Queen: 'O Hamlet, speak no more.
Thou turn'st mine eyes into my very soul,
And there I see such black and grainèd spots ...'
Hamlet, Act III, scene iv.

Mary, William's mother, who died in 1608, is a shadowy figure. However, in *Hamlet* (1600-02) William created a striking mother-son relationship between Hamlet and his mother Gertrude, who had remarried.

Printed Plays

Titus Andronicus, the first of William's plays to be published, was printed in 1594. His name was not even on the title page: clearly, he was not yet famous enough to be worth mentioning.

Many more of William's plays were published during his lifetime. He made little money out of them because the scripts belonged to his company, not to himself.

*Shakespeare on film: Anthony Hopkins takes the lead role in the 1999 film adaptation of **Titus Andronicus**.*

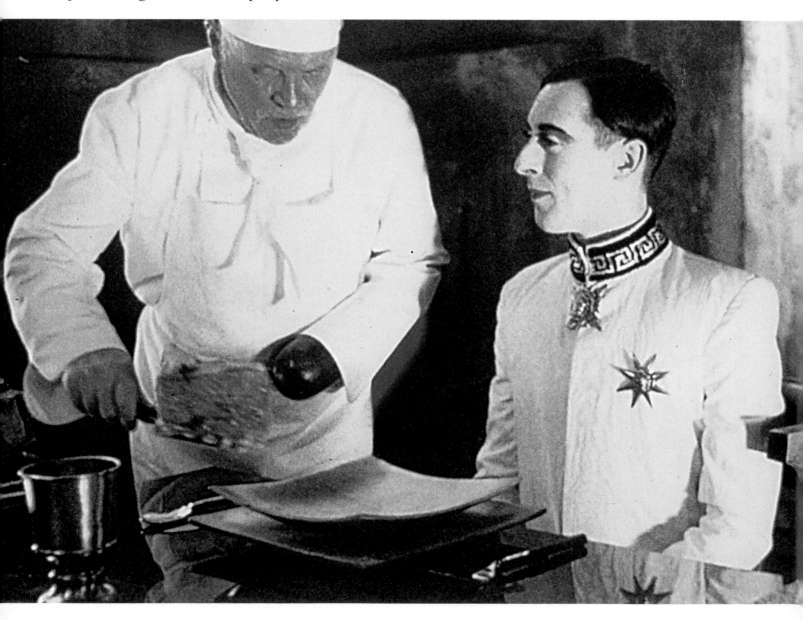

MR. WILLIAM
SHAKESPEARES
COMEDIES,
HISTORIES, &
TRAGEDIES.

Publifhed according to the True Originall Copies.

Martin Droefhout fculpfit London

LONDON

The cover of the First Folio, the first collected works of William Shakespeare, 1623. The picture is the only contemporary one of him we have.

Most of these early editions of the plays are full of mistakes and inaccuracies. Some were written from actors' memories. Once a play was written, the individual parts were copied out and given to the actors. This was to stop rival companies getting hold of the entire script and putting on their own productions.

William's final versions of his plays do not exist. The texts used today have been put together by scholars from the sixteenth and seventeenth century editions.

Hamlet's 'To be, or not to be' speech is probably William's most famous piece of writing. When it was first printed, it looked quite different from the version we use today (see panel).

**'To be, or not to be, I there's the point,
To die, to sleepe, is that all?'**
First Quarto

**'To be, or not to be: that is the question:
Whether 'tis nobler in the mind to suffer
The slings and arrows of outrageous fortune ...'**
Hamlet, Act III, scene i.

Love on Stage

Relationships between men and women lie at the heart of many of William's plays. In his early plays, especially *Romeo and Juliet* (1594-96), William presents love as a disease: something that 'afflicts' people, especially the young. This suggests that he saw it as something to be avoided, which was a common view in his day. Was he speaking from his own experience with Anne Hathaway?

In 1616, William left Anne his second best bed in his will. Some scholars believe William had a girlfriend in Oxford whom he visited on his journeys from London to Stratford.

*Leonardo DiCaprio and Claire Danes in a popular modern film of **Romeo and Juliet** directed by Baz Luhrmann in 1996.*

In *Othello* (1604) and *The Winter's Tale* (1610-11) William explores the destructive power of jealousy. Othello is a successful general who kills his wife when he is tricked into believing she has been unfaithful to him. Leontes, the King of Sicily in *The Winter's Tale,* sends his wife to prison convinced she has had an affair and refuses to believe her newborn child is his.

Iago: 'O, beware, my lord, of jealousy!
It is the green-eyed monster, which doth mock
The meat it feeds on.'
Othello, Act III, scene iii.

*Paul Robeson in 1942 in the title role of **Othello**, William's brilliant study of jealousy.*

'His Elder Days'

The form of most of William's plays is similar to that of others of his time: comedies were lighter plays, often involving misunderstandings, like William's *Much Ado About Nothing* (1598-99) and Thomas Dekker's *The Shoemaker's Holiday*; tragedies were serious, often sad plays about human weaknesses, like William's *King Lear* (1605-06) and Christopher Marlowe's *Doctor Faustus* and history plays were based on real-life events, like William's *Richard III* (1592-93) and Marlowe's *Edward II*.

As he grew older, William's plays became more mysterious. Features of comedy and tragedy are mixed together in a way not seen before. This is most clear in his last great play, *The Tempest* (1611).

> '... in his elder days [he] lived at Stratford, and supplied the stage with two plays every year, and for that had an allowance so large, that he spent at the rate of £1,000 a year, as I have heard.'
> John Ward, vicar of Stratford, cited in Russ McDonald, *The Bedford Companion to Shakespeare*.

A fanciful Victorian painting of William and his friends in the early seventeenth century.

An illustration (1909) by Arthur Rackham for William's magical last full play, **The Tempest.** *Rackham shows the 'voices' of the spirits, which are described by Caliban in Act III, scene ii.*

The scene is set on an 'enchanted isle', full of magic and music, where sinners are punished and repent their wicked ways. By this time William was spending more time in Stratford. After *The Tempest* he virtually retired, writing only two more works (*Henry VIII* in 1612-13 and *The Two Noble Kinsmen* in 1613), in collaboration with others.

When Prospero, *The Tempest*'s main character, says these words at the end of the play it is almost as if the playwright himself is saying farewell.

> 'I'll break my staff,
> Bury it certain fathoms in the earth,
> And deeper than did ever plummet sound
> I'll drown my book.'
> (*The Tempest,* Act V, scene i).

41

The 'Merry Meeting'

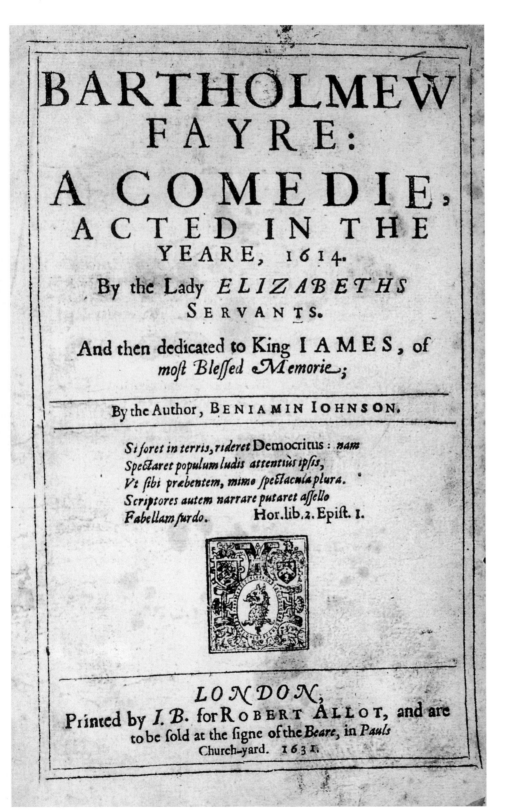

BARTHOLMEW FAYRE: A COMEDIE, ACTED IN THE YEARE, 1614. By the Lady ELIZABETHS SERVANTS.

And then dedicated to King IAMES, of most Blessed Memorie;

By the Author, BENIAMIN IOHNSON.

Si foret in terris, rideret Democritus : nam
Spectaret populum ludis attentius ipsis,
Vt sibi præbentem, mimo spectacula plura.
Scriptores autem narrare putaret asello
Fabellam surdo.   Hor. lib. 2. Epist. 1.

LONDON,
Printed by I. B. for ROBERT ALLOT, and are
to be sold at the signe of the Beare, in Pauls
Church-yard. 1631.

In 1614 William was fortunate to escape serious loss when a ferocious fire ravaged the town of Stratford.

Early in 1616, perhaps sensing that his end was near, William changed his will. He ensured that the property left to his daughter Judith would not be taken by her disreputable husband, Thomas Quiney. Shortly after this, John Ward said that William drank too much at a meeting with his theatrical friends, the poet Michael Drayton and the playwright Ben Jonson.

After this 'merry meeting' William caught a fever and died on 23 April 1616, the same date that he is believed to have been born.

A poster for Ben Jonson's popular comedy Bartholmew Fayre, 1614.

> *'Good friend for Jesus' sake forbear,*
> *To dig the dust enclosèd here:*
> *Blessed be the man that spares these stones,*
> *And cursed be he that moves my bones.'*
> The words that are carved into the stone on Willliam's grave.

He was buried in Holy Trinity church, Stratford, where he had been baptised 52 years earlier. Over his grave a stone slab was placed, on which was carved a curse on whoever disturbed his bones. His last wish has been observed, and his remains have lain undisturbed ever since.

The monument to William Shakespeare in the Holy Trinity church, Stratford-upon-Avon where he is buried.

'Soul of the Age!'

'I, therefore, will begin. Soul of the Age!
The applause, delight, the wonder of our Stage!
My Shakespeare, rise ...'
Ben Jonson in *To the Memory of my Beloved*
Mr. William Shakespeare.

For William's reputation to survive his death, a reliable collection of all his works was needed. In 1623 this was done by a group of his former friends and colleagues. Known as the *First Folio*, it contained all his plays (except *Henry VIII* (1612-13)) under the title 'Mr William Shakespeare's Comedies, Histories and Tragedies'.

International appeal: Umabatha – *The Zulu Macbeth* – was performed on the Globe stage in 1997.

Since then all the plays have been read and performed every year throughout the English-speaking world. They have been translated into virtually every language, too. Most have been adapted for the cinema. Many have been re-written in other forms: the musical *West Side Story*, for example, is based on *Romeo and Juliet* (1594-96).

No other playwright has received such praise and admiration. In a famous poem, Ben Jonson described William as the 'soul of the age'. Nowadays, seeing how his reputation has grown, we might prefer to call him the soul of all humankind.

Inspiration for others: a scene from a 1961 production of **West Side Story,** *the hit musical based on* **William's** *Romeo and Juliet.*

Glossary

ado Matter or business.

blank verse Non-rhyming text.

coat of arms Symbols representing a family.

earl A title of nobility.

enchanted Magical, under a spell.

gatherer Someone who collected entry money at the door of a playhouse.

half-timbered A building built on a massive wooden frame.

iambic pentameter A line of verse containing 5 iambic feet where the syllable stress is weak and then strong.

patron Someone who supports a talented but poorer person or group of people.

patron saint A saint chosen to guard over a country.

playhouse A theatre.

poach To steal animals.

puritan Someone who wanted to rid the Church of England of all traces of the Roman Catholic church, such as bishops and holy statues.

script Words of a play.

shareholder Someone who puts money into a business in order to get more money back when it makes a profit.

sonnet A poem of fourteen lines.

tragedy A play in which the leading character gets into trouble (and usually dies) because of a fault in their character.

troupe A group.

verse Poetry.

yeoman A middle-class farmer.

Further Information

Places of Interest

Shakespeare's plays are regularly staged all over the world. Among the most impressive are productions at the Globe Theatre, London, by the Royal Shakespeare Company, at the Shakespeare Memorial Theatre, Stratford-upon-Avon and in London, and the Theatre Festival in Stratford, Ontario, Canada.

In Stratford-upon-Avon one can visit Shakespeare's birthplace, Anne Hathaway's Cottage, New Place and Halls Croft (where Susanna and her husband John Hall lived).

In Wilmcote, near Stratford, is the timber-framed farmhouse in which William's mother Mary may have been born.

The Shakespeare Centre, Henley Street, Stratford-upon-Avon has valuable exhibitions, as does The Globe Theatre, London.

Books

Peter Chrisp, *Eyewitness: Shakespeare*, Dorling Kindersley, 2002

Wendy Greenhill, *Shakespeare's Theatre*, Heinemann, 2000

Roni Jay, *Shakespeare: a Beginner's Guide*, Headway, 2000

Stewart Ross, *William Shakespeare*, Evans, 1999

Sources

John Aubrey, *Brief Lives*, Penguin, 1976

G.B Harrison, *Introducing Shakespeare*, Penguin, 1991

Russ McDonald, *The Bedford Companion to Shakespeare*, Macmillan, 1966

Date Chart

1558 Elizabeth I becomes Queen of England.

1564 William Shakespeare born in Stratford-upon-Avon.

1567 The first purpose-built playhouse was built in London.

1582 Marries Anne Hathaway.

1583 Susanna Shakespeare born.

1585 Hamnet and Judith Shakespeare (twins) born.

1588-90 Comes to London.

1592 Writing *The Comedy of Errors* (his first known full play), *Richard III*.

1593 London theatres closed. Writing *The Taming of the Shrew*, *The Rape of Lucrece* (a poem) and his sonnets.

1595 With the Lord Chamberlain's Men. *Richard II* performed.

1596 Becomes a gentleman and gets a coat of arms. Hamnet dies.

1597 Buys New Place in Stratford. Writing *The Merchant of Venice*.

1598-9 Writing *Much Ado About Nothing*.

1599 The Globe Theatre opens. Writing *Henry V*.

1600-2 Writing *As You Like It*, *Hamlet* and *Twelfth Night*.

1601 John Shakespeare dies.

1602 Buys land in Stratford.

1603 Queen Elizabeth I dies and James VI of Scotland becomes James I of England. Lord Chamberlain's Men become the King's Men.

1605-6 Writing *King Lear* and *Macbeth*.

1606-7 Writing *Antony and Cleopatra*.

1608 King's Men start using Blackfriars playhouse. William's mother dies.

1609 The Sonnets published.

1610-11 Writing *The Winter's Tale*.

1611 *The Tempest*, his last full play, is performed. Spending more time in Stratford.

1616 William Shakespeare dies.

1623 First Folio edition of plays published.